Space Mania

DISCOVERING DISTANT WORLDS
WITHOUT LEAVING YOUR OWN

Michael A. DiSpezio

Sterling Publishing Co., Inc.
New York

Photo credits
Page 8: Spiral galaxy image courtesy of NASA
Page 12: Andromeda Galaxy image courtesy of NASA
Page 37: Moon surface image courtesy of USGS Astrogeology Research Program
Page 80: Author's photo by Tony DiSpezio

Edited by Hazel Chan
Designed by Nancy B. Field

Library of Congress Cataloging-in-Publication Data

Dispezio, Michael A.
   Space mania / Michael A. DiSpezio.
      v. cm.
Includes index.
Summary: Provides a history of the Universe, a look at galaxies, constellations, stars, and space-related activities. Contents: Blasting Off – The Big Picture – Heaps of Stars – Big Bang – Seeing Galaxies – A Galaxy of Our Own – Center of Our System – Daily Spin – Seasonal Errors – Up Close and Personal – A Foreign Dish – Beam Me Up – Big Ears – Aliens Among Us? – Home Planet – Meet the Moon – Scope It Out – Craters – Moon Phases – Shadow Games (Solar Eclipse) – Wanderers – Squished Circles – Inner Planets – Outer Planets – A Model System – Distances in the System – Black Holes – What's a Kid to Do? – Dividing up the Sky – The North Star – Bedroom Constellations – Finding Constellations – Stars Down Under – Moving On – Flashes of Light – A Yearly Shower – Blowing in the Wind – The Final Frontier.
   ISBN 0-8069-7287-4
   1. Astronomy–Juvenile literature. 2. Outer space–Juvenile literature. [1. Astronomy. 2. Outer space.]
I. Title.
   QB46 .D57 2003
   520–dc21   2002008493

10 9 8 7 6 5 4 3 2 1

Published in paperback 2004 by Sterling Publishing Co., Inc.
387 Park Avenue South, New York, NY 10016

© 2003 by Michael A. DiSpezio

Distributed in Canada by Sterling Publishing
℅ Canadian Manda Group, One Atlantic Avenue, Suite 105
Toronto, Ontario, Canada M6K 3E7
Distributed in Great Britain by Chris Lloyd at Orca Book
Services, Stanley House, Fleets Lane, Poole BH15 3AJ, England
Distributed in Australia by Capricorn Link (Australia) Pty. Ltd.
P.O. Box 704, Windsor, NSW 2756, Australia

Printed in China

Sterling ISBN 0-8069-7287-4 Hardcover
           ISBN 1-4027-1772-5 Paperback

Table of Contents

Blasting Off

Do you ever wish that you could travel through space? You know the scene: a huge spacecraft, gravity engine, and the ability to blast by stars and planets at thousands of miles per hour!

Well, guess what? You are. Although it may not feel it, you're rocking and rolling on a voyage through the universe.

Look down. That nonmoving ground beneath your feet isn't so nonmoving. That's because it's attached to a huge spaceship. This craft has a name. Perhaps you've heard of it? It's called Earth.

Earth doesn't sit still. It spins. It moves around the Sun. It circles the center of our Milky Way Galaxy. And since it formed, our planet has been moving away from the spot where our universe first began.

Sounds interesting? You bet it is. And there's more, much more. So kick back, fasten your seat belts, and prepare to blast off into the cool and far out universe of *Space Mania*.

The Big Picture

The universe is a big place, a VERY BIG place. In fact, it's the ultimate big place. It's the cosmic parking lot for everything that exists.

Okay, so what shape does the universe have? No one knows. However, many scientists think that the entire universe exists on the surface of some super gigantic ball. Nothing exists inside this ball and nothing exists beyond its curved surface.

Scientists believe that the farthest point from anywhere to anywhere in the universe is 14 billion light years. Imagine 14 billion light years! That certainly sounds impressive, especially if you don't have a clue what a light year is. Okay, let's take it back a step.

What is a light year?

a) Twelve months without chores, exams, or homework.

b) A year with only 362 days.

c) The distance that a beam of light travels in one year.

ANSWER: c) The distance that a beam of light travels in one year. Although it sounds like a unit of time, a light year is actually a measure of distance. Light travels at the incredible speed of 186,000 miles per second. For those of you living in metric countries, your light travels at 300,000 kilometers per second. Either way, it's a very fast speed.

Follow me. Every second, a beam of light covers 186,000 miles (300,000 km). Seconds add up. In a minute, that beam of light will have traveled over 11 million miles (over 17 million kilometers). Can you imagine how far a light beam can travel in a year? Don't hurt yourself. We'll tell you. In one year a beam of light covers nearly 6 trillion miles (over 9 trillion kilometers).

Cool Fact

It takes light around 12 hours to go from one end of our solar system to the other.

Heaps of Stars

It's nighttime. Look up and what do you see? If it's the ceiling, move outside. Now, look up again. This time, if the sky is clear and there isn't too much light pollution, you can see stars—as many as 2500 of them on a clear, perfect night.

But not all of the tiny bright dots in the sky are stars. For now, let's forget about the jets, satellites, birthday balloons, and other "down to Earth" objects. We'll even overlook planets. The space objects we'll focus on are called galaxies (gal-ACKS-ees).

Galaxies are huge heaps of stars. Some contain up to 5000 billion stars. However, since they are so far away, all those stars appear as a single dot. So the next time you look into the sky, remember that some of those stars aren't single stars at all. They are billions of stars!

Spiral galaxy

CLOSER LOOK

With your eyes alone, you can't see much. However, when people who study the sky examine these distant objects using high-powered telescopes, they uncover shape and structure. These sky watchers are called astronomers.

Since you probably don't live in an observatory (because if you did, you wouldn't need to buy this book), let's see what galaxies look like.

Galaxies come in three basic shapes. Some look like a random mess of stars. Others are round or oval-like concentrations of stars. Still others have a pinwheel-like shape and are called spiral galaxies.

IN A SEA OF NOTHING

Galaxies are sometimes called island universes. Like islands, they are separated from other galaxies by a huge sea. But the sea that divides the galaxies isn't made of water. In fact, most of it hardly contains anything at all. Scientists call this empty space a vacuum (VAK-que-mm).

Irregular

Oval

Spiral

from top

from side

Big Bang

Galaxies are moving away from us! It's nothing personal. They were set in motion by an explosion that occurred some time between 10 billion to 20 billion years ago.

From studying the light given off by distant galaxies, astronomers think our universe began with a tremendous blast. They call this event the Big Bang.

At the moment of the Big Bang, the entire universe was packed into space that was much, much smaller than the period at the end of this sentence.

Then, it happened. The universe exploded into existence.

As the universe expanded, its energy was changed into matter. Suddenly, empty space was getting stuffed with things like protons, neutrons, and electrons.

MODEL THE BIG BANG

You can make a model of the expanding universe with a balloon and a marker. Here's how:

1. Use a marker to draw spirals across the surface of an empty balloon. These circles represent galaxies.

2. Put on safety goggles. Inflate the balloon halfway. This model represents the universe as it was 7 billion years ago.

3. Keep inflating the balloon until it is full. Now you've reached a model of the current universe size. Tie up the end of the balloon.

Mind Boggler

Inside the shell of our expanding universe is nothing. It is past history where the universe once was. All things in the present exist on the skin of the balloon. The space outside of the enlarging shell is the future. Strange, eh?

Seeing Galaxies

Imagine that it is nighttime. You step outside and begin exploring the evening sky. Your first mission is to find the Milky Way. This, however, isn't much of a challenge since we live in the Milky Way Galaxy. Most anywhere you look is a part of our home galaxy.

However, when sky watchers say "Milky Way," they are talking about a band of light that crosses the evening sky. The "milky" appearance of this band is caused by the large concentration of stars and dust in this part of our galaxy.

SOMETHING IMPRESSIVE?

Okay, so you want to see something that will impress your teacher? How about a distant galaxy? The easiest galaxy to see is the great Andromeda Galaxy.

Andromeda Galaxy

The Andromeda Galaxy is located in a region of space called the Andromeda Constellation. Check out the star map below. Finding the Great Square, Cassiopeia, or Pegasus may help you locate this galaxy.

Like many sky objects, the Andromeda Galaxy is only visible part of the year. In order to find it, you'll need to search the Northern sky from August through January.

During this time, the Andromeda Galaxy stands out among its dim neighbors.

The Andromeda Galaxy is about 2 million light years away. Even so, just an ordinary pair of binoculars is all you need to make out the galaxy's basic shape. As you'll see, Andromeda has a bright center surrounded by a cloud-like glow.

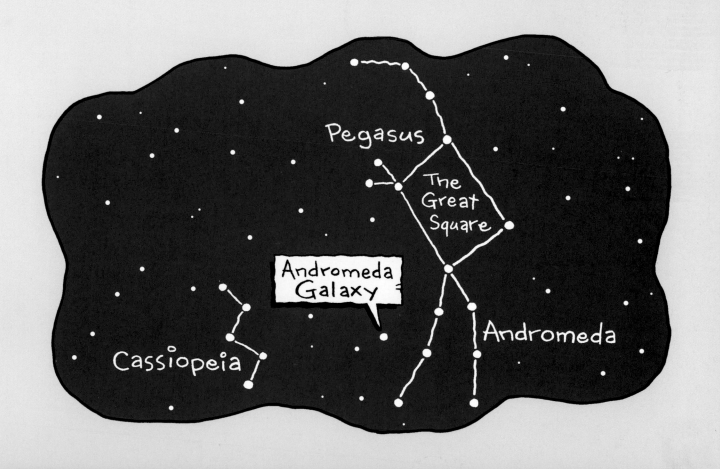

A Galaxy of Our Own

Our Sun is one of about 200 billion stars in the Milky Way Galaxy. Although no one has ever been outside the Milky Way (or even close), we can tell it's a spiral from the arrangement of stars we see from Earth.

The middle of the spiral has a star-packed center called the *central bulge*. Attached to this bulge are four arms that trail off into space. Each arm is filled with millions of stars. Our Sun is in the Orion (Oh-ryan) arm.

The Milky Way spins like a giant pinwheel. It takes our Sun about 220 million years to complete one lap. Astronomers think that our Sun has probably made twenty-five laps around the galactic center since the Milky Way formed.

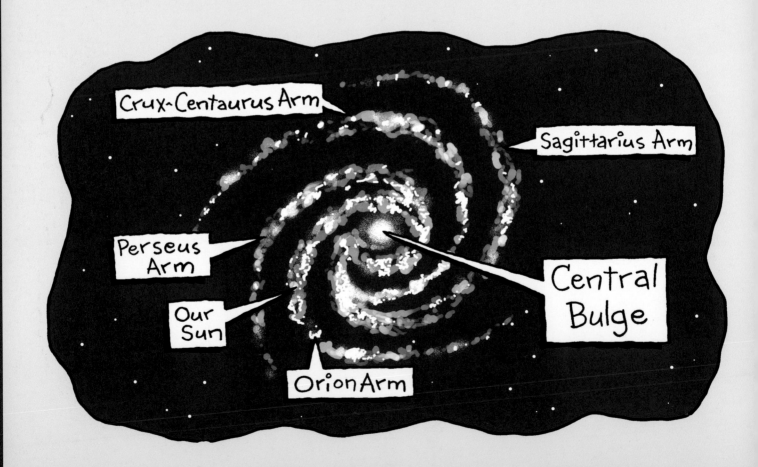

Crux-Centaurus Arm

Sagittarius Arm

Perseus Arm

Our Sun

Central Bulge

Orion Arm

BUILD A MODEL

Okay, it's your turn to make your own Milky Way.

You'll Need

Cotton
Toothpicks
Clay
Paint
Sparkles
Old shoe box

Use these materials to build a shoe-box model of the Milky Way. Don't forget to label each part and show the location of our Sun.

Center of Our System

Like all stars, our Sun is a huge ball of glowing gases. The gases glow because they are hot—EXTREMELY HOT. This heat is created by the nuclear reactions that occur deep inside the Sun's center.

WHAT'S COOKING (IN THE NUCLEAR OVEN)?

Matter. Within the center of the Sun, awesome temperatures produce nuclear reactions. During these reactions, atoms combine together to form larger particles.

As these particles form, something gets lost, really lost . . . as in annihilated (AN-eye-oll-a-ted) lost. Gone. No more. Wiped out.

The small amount of matter that gets annihilated is changed into a tremendous amount of energy. That's the reaction that's at the center of every shining star.

NUCLEAR

NUCLEAR Cooking

HOW BIG IS OUR SUN?

Borrow a large handful of pennies. You'll need 109 to be precise. Each penny represents the width of one Earth.

Arrange the pennies in a straight line so they are positioned end-to-end. This whole line of pennies represents the width of the Sun.

Fill It Up

If Earth was a gumball and the Sun was a cosmic gumball machine, the machine would be filled with over one million Earths.

LIVING IN THE PAST

The Sun is about 93 million miles (about 150 million kilometers) from Earth. If you do some math, you'll find that it takes light about 8 minutes to journey from this star's surface to the Earth. Therefore, the Sun's image that you see is actually 8 minutes old. It's past history.

Think about it. If some evil alien blew up the Sun, this star would still look the same for a short while. We wouldn't see any change until the light from the explosion reached Earth.

Daily Spin

Like a top, the Earth spins on its axis. It is this movement that produces night and day. If you want to impress an adult, use the word "rotation" (ro-TAY-shun) to describe this spinning motion.

The top-like spin makes it appear as if the Sun rises in the east and sets in the west. However, it is the Earth that is doing the moving. The rotation is like clockwork—it always stays the same. In fact, you can build a simple clock based upon this motion.

But First, A Word of Caution
Never look directly at the Sun! Its light can injure your eyes and cause permanent blindness.

BUILDING A SUNDIAL

You'll Need
Heavy stock paper
Markers
Scissors
Glue or tape
Thread
Watch

1. Copy the pattern shown on the opposite page. You can either photocopy it and paste it onto a piece of heavy-stock backing or you can simply draw it on sturdy paper.
2. Use scissors to carefully cut out the large rectangular shape.
3. Fold the clock along the dotted line.
4. Use glue or tape to attach a piece of thread from the middle of the top edge to the middle of the bottom edge.

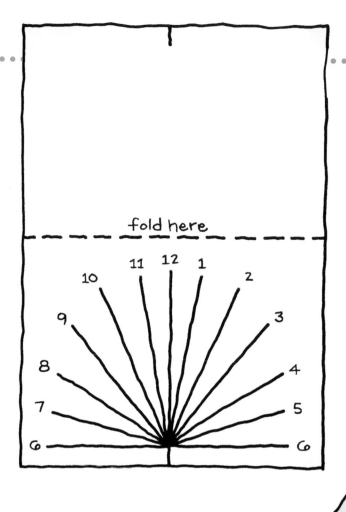

fold here

10   11   12   1   2

9   3

8   4

7   5

6   6

5. Use a watch to find out the local time. Then, position this sundial so that the shadow falls on that time line. Once it's set, don't move it. That's all there is to it. As the day goes on, the Sun's shadow will move across the hour lines.

Don't Set Your Clock to It

This sundial that you built is not "tweaked" for your location. If you want the time to be accurate, you need to adjust the dial's position based on your distance from the equator.

Seasonal Errors

The Earth is closest to the Sun during which season: summer or winter?

Summer. Sounds logical, but too bad it is not correct. Don't feel alone. Most college graduates think the same way.

Winter. Sounds crazy, but it's true. Summer and winter have nothing to do with the distance between the Sun and Earth.

CONCENTRATING ON A CURVE

Borrow a desktop globe and spin it. As you can see, the axis isn't straight up and down. There's a tilt to the spin. As the Earth moves around the Sun, the tilt remains pointed in the same direction. Since the Earth isn't straight up and down, the amount of light isn't the same across the Earth's surface. During the summer in the Northern Hemisphere, there is a greater amount of sunlight falling on the top half of the Earth. This concentrated light produces higher temperatures.

During winter in the Northern Hemisphere, that same beam of sunlight gets spread out over a larger area. The result is cooler temperatures.

If you live south of the equator, it's the same thing but the timing is reversed.

DON'T TAKE OUR WORD FOR IT

Check it out yourself. Get a desktop globe and a small flashlight. Position the globe so that the lower half (Southern Hemisphere) is angled closer to the flashlight. Hold the flashlight horizontally. Aim the flashlight beam directly at the Earth. Observe the concentrated spot of light that appears on the lower half of the Earth. This concentrated beam produces summer south of the equator. Raise and lower the flashlight while keeping the beam level. Can you see how the beam spreads out more over the curved surface of the Northern Hemisphere? With less concentrated sunlight, the Northern Hemisphere experiences colder temperatures.

Up Close and Personal

With your eyes alone, all the stars and galaxies look like a blur of light. To improve their image, you need to get up close and personal. You can do that with either a telescope or a pair of binoculars.

BINOCULARS

Although they aren't as powerful as telescopes, binoculars are easy to use, portable, and most likely someone you know already owns a pair. What could be easier?

Most binoculars have numbers printed on their case, such as 7×35. The "7" refers to the magnifying power. The "35" refers to the size of the lens. The larger this lens, the better the binoculars are at finding dim sky objects.

TELESCOPE TYPES

Although there are a few types of telescopes, we'll just mention the refracting telescope. This model looks like a big tube with lenses on either end. The lens closest to your eye is called the eyepiece. The lens furthest away is the objective.

Before you buy a telescope, research the models and features you need. Check out astronomy magazines or go on-line and search for product reviews. By doing so, you can become an informed consumer and make a better purchase.

Objective Lens

Eyepiece

Focusing Ring

Focusing Knob

Eyepiece

Focus Adjustment Ring

What to Look For

A good entry-level telescope will have up to 100 times magnification. At this power, you should be able to see the polar ice caps of Mars and Jupiter's main cloud belts!

As the magnification goes up, however, the image can get fuzzy. Therefore a 100-power telescope may be a better choice if it shows more detail than a poorer quality 300-power model. It is more important to get a clearer, cleaner image.

Plus, don't forget about the stand. As the magnification goes up, the image jumps and jitters. To view a stable image, you need a stable platform.

Objective Lens

Mount

Tripod

A Foreign Dish

Have you seen the movie *Contact* or *GoldenEye*? If so, you were treated to a view of the world's largest radio telescope. This huge device is found at the Arecibo (Ahr-E-see-bow) Observatory in Puerto Rico.

The large dish is made up of almost 40,000 aluminum panels. These panels collect faint radio signals and reflect them at hanging antennas. The signals picked up by the antennas are transferred to radios, amplifiers, and other electronic devices.

Perhaps you are wondering, "Why bother with radio waves when you can easily see light waves?" Good question. The answer is that many space objects give off more radio waves than light waves. Without studying their radio signals, these objects would be mostly undetected. Plus, by studying both visible and radio signals, scientists can learn much more about space objects.

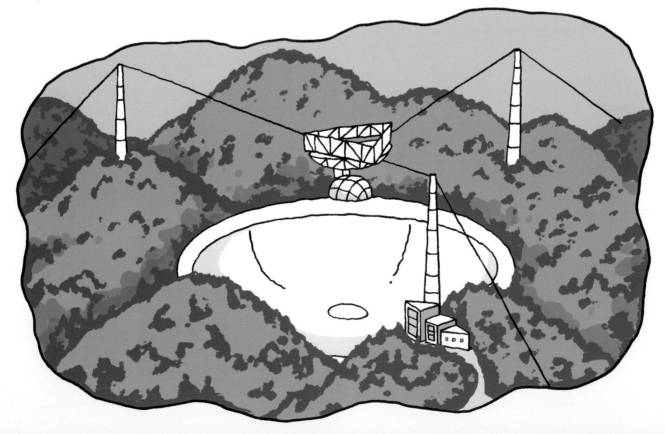

A DISH OF YOUR OWN

You can build a dish antenna using a metal wok lid or a large shallow bowl wrapped in aluminum foil. Take your TV remote control and stand at the opposite end of the room from the TV. Aim the inner curve of the bowl at the TV. Be sure not to stand in front of the bowl.

Point your remote control directly at the center of the bowl. It should be about 1 foot (30 cm) from the bowl's center. As you press the control's buttons, a signal leaves the control unit and strikes the bowl's inner surface. The reflected and concentrated signal reverses direction and heads toward the TV. If your signal doesn't control the TV, adjust the position of the controller and the angle of the bowl. Don't give up. Eventually, you'll create a signal beam that operates the TV!

Beam Me Up

Tonight, take a flashlight outdoors and aim it at some distant star. Flip on the light for about a second, then turn it off. You've just created a beam of light that is traveling skyward at 186,000 miles (300,000 km) per second.

Your beam has a beginning and an end. The front end of the beam was created when you flipped on the switch. The back end of the beam formed when you turned the flashlight off.

Although it is cool to think that some day your beam will arrive at its alien target, it won't. As it travels, the beam spreads out. Eventually, like a ripple in a pond, the beam will have spread out so far that it is no longer a beam of light. But it's a cool concept to think about.

To get around the spread of light, astronomers blast radio waves into space. Flashlights are replaced by gigantic radio telescopes that are set to "transmit" signals, not receive them. Radio signals produced by these transmitters don't spread out. In fact, astronomers hope that some day an alien civilization will receive and decode these messages. What then? No one knows.

Radio Telescope

FIGURE IT OUT

Here's a signal that was sent out into space by the Arecibo dish back in 1974. Suppose you were an alien who intercepted it. Could you locate symbols in this message that represent the subjects below?

The Arecibo dish from where the message was sent.

A representation of DNA.

The sun with nine planets (with Earth moved to the side).

The numbers 1–10 (represented in a binary code).

A human.

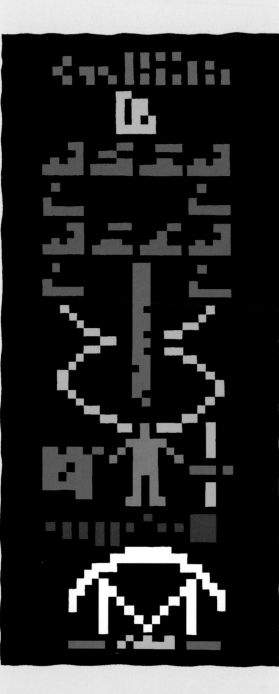

Big Ears

SETI, short for the Search for Extraterrestrial Intelligence, is made up of dozens of projects that are aimed at uncovering evidence of alien civilizations. One SETI program searches the sky for alien radio signals that would prove that *we are not alone.* Another SETI program searches space for beams of laser light.

WOW!

In 1977, the radio telescope at Ohio State detected a radio signal that was unlike any other signal ever picked up by a radio telescope. Not only was it a very strong signal, but it came from somewhere in outer space. The military and NASA reported that there were no known satellites in that part of the sky that might have produced the signal. This signal was so "unmistakably strong" that one of the scientists wrote the word "Wow" on the computer printout! In fact, this encounter is known as the "Wow signal."

Too bad the signal didn't repeat. After 37 seconds, the signal could no longer be detected! Some astronomers believe that the telescope detected a sweep of a radio beam sent out by a distant civilization. A moment later when the same region of space was examined, the radio signal was no longer there.

THE DRAKE EQUATION

It's a numbers game. Astronomer Frank Drake developed an equation that could be used to estimate the number of alien civilizations that might have the ability to communicate with Earth. It's an impressive equation that considers all sorts of things, from the rate of star formation to the time that a civilization remains intact before getting wiped out. Using his equation, Drake estimates that there are about 10,000 planets within our galaxy that have the ability to communicate across interstellar space. Remember that it's only a guess, his guess. What's yours?

Drake's Equation

$$N = R \times f_p \times n_e \times f_l \times f_i \times f_c \times L$$

EARTH

Aliens Among Us?

Most likely, you've heard of UFOs, Unidentified Flying Objects. The abbreviation is meant to describe spaceships of alien origin. Ooooooooo. In the real world, however, it includes almost everything from swamp gas to garbage can lids.

So far, scientists don't have real proof that aliens have visited our planet (or are not willing to admit these encounters). The facts just don't seem to support aliens living among us. UFO sightings can often be explained by natural phenomena or hoaxes. However, to many people, it is much more exciting to believe that Earth is some all-season destination on the alien tourist circuit.

ROSWELL

In 1947, something crashed in Roswell, New Mexico. The army, who recovered the crash debris, first announced that it had found a "flying disk." Needless to say, everyone was excited about the discovery of an alien craft. How much cooler could this get? The following day, however, the army changed its story and said that what it really found was a weather balloon. Ugh, how boring.

Believers in the "close encounter" version said that the balloon story was a cover-up! All sorts of tales soon spread about alien bodies that were recovered from the crash site. Some people said that aliens were brought to the Groom Lake military base. You probably have heard of this ultra top-secret military base by its more common name, Area 51.

WHAT'S UP WITH AREA 51?

Although the military now says that the crash debris was wreckage from a "spy balloon," the secrecy surrounding Area 51 keeps the mystery alive. Perhaps you are wondering why they are so secretive if they have nothing to hide? Actually, they do have things to hide. Area 51 is a remote air base that for years has been used for all sorts of experimental aircraft and weapons. It's even been the home to spy planes, including the U-2 and SR-71 Blackbird.

To maintain our national security, the military needs to keep what happens at this base under wraps. They say they can't give the public access to their top-secret records—or is this explanation just another cover-up? Most likely, we'll never know for certain. However, most scientists believe that aliens never crash-landed in the Nevada desert.

Welcome To ROSWELL New Mexico

Home Planet

Imagine a couple of alien astronomers on a distant planet. Like the Earth-bound variety, these sky watchers have incredible telescopes that can detect and analyze light from distant galaxies.

On this night, the aliens focus on an average star in the Orion arm. They are especially interested in the third planet of this system. Carefully, they study this planet in their telescope. Success. From what they observe, both agree that this blue planet has life.

Okay, so what was it? What earthly action creates evidence of life that can be seen from across the galaxy?

a) Cities that light up at night.
b) Forests that cover much of the land.
c) Cows that pass gas.

ANSWER: c) Cows that pass gas—and we're not kidding. This signal begins when cows eat grass. As they digest this plant material,

they create a good deal of methane (METH-ane) gas. In fact, most of the methane that enters our atmosphere is a result of animal digestion.

Methane that enters the atmosphere reacts with other gases. But since cows continually eat grass, there is always methane in the air. Because this gas can be seen by special telescopes, it suggests some sort of ongoing life process.

EARTH CENTERED

If our two alien friends observed the Earth and the Moon, they'd call us a double-planet system. That's because the Moon is large enough to be a planet on its own. However, since we live on Earth, we don't split the planetary billing. *We* are the planet. The Moon is only the Moon.

Meet the Moon

The dark splotches on the Moon's surface are:

a) Unsightly age spots
(about 4 billion years old).

b) Paved parking lots.

c) Seas.

ANSWER: c) Seas. However, don't go looking for any water. The Moon is a completely dry place with no H_2O to be found anywhere.

Okay, so if there's no water on the surface, what dimwit would call it a sea? That "dimwit" was a guy named Galileo Galilei. Perhaps you've heard of him?

When Galileo first observed the Moon, he noticed that its surface was divided into light and dark areas. Like the rest of us, he made mistakes. He thought those dark areas were seas. He called each one a *mare*, which is the Latin word for sea. The name stuck.

These days we know that the "seas" are areas of solid dark surface. The darkness comes from the minerals that are in this rock. Unlike the lighter surface, the seas were formed when liquid rock that flowed from lunar volcanoes became solid.

Galileo also observed the Moon's mountains and highlands. He noticed that the surface was covered with pits. These pits are called craters. Most of the craters were produced by large chunks of space rock that struck the lunar surface soon after the Moon formed.

MOON MAKING

Scientists have several theories on how the Moon got there. Check out the ones below. Can you uncover the imposter?

a) The Moon was an interplanetary wanderer. It went all over the solar system. As it whizzed by Earth, it got caught up in our gravity. The rest is history.

b) The Moon formed at the same time as the Earth. As our nearest neighbor, it came together from its own glob of cooling space soup.

c) The Moon is the cooled-off core of our Sun's twin (and evil) sister.

d) When the Earth was forming, it collided with a huge chunk of space garbage. That impact knocked out a huge piece of our planet that became the Moon.

Answer on page 79.

Scope It Out

The Moon is an easy target to explore. Using a pair of binoculars, you can observe all sorts of lunar features.

To get a better "overall" picture of the Moon, check it out at different times of the month. As time goes by, the changing angle of sunlight will highlight different parts of the surface.

Did you know that a bad time to view the Moon is during a full Moon? At that time, the angle of sunshine doesn't create dramatic shadows. This makes the surface appear flat and featureless.

How many of the following craters and mares can you locate?

Craters:

1. Crater Tycho
2. Crater Copernicus
3. Crater Plato

Dark Areas:

4. Oceanus Procellarum (Ocean of Storms)
5. Mare Frigoris (Sea of Cold)
6. Mare Imbrium (Sea of Rains)
7. Mare Serenitatis (Sea of Serenity)
8. Mare Tranquillitatis (Sea of Tranquility)
9. Mare Crisium (Sea of Crises)
10. Mare Fecunditatis (Sea of Fertility)
11. Mare Nectaris (Sea of Nectar)
12. Mare Nubium (Sea of Clouds)
13. Mare Humorum (Sea of Moisture)
14. Mare Vaporum (Sea of Vapors)

Craters

Most of the craters that we see on the Moon were made over 4 billion years ago. At that time, the Moon's surface was constantly being hit by all sorts of space rocks. Since the Moon lacks an atmosphere, the rocks didn't burn up as they fell to the surface. Instead, they slammed into the Moon, creating millions of holes called impact craters.

MAKE A CRATER

Let's explore how impacts create craters.

You'll Need

A large bowl	Ruler
Flour	Safety goggles
Two marbles	

1. Fill a large bowl about halfway with flour. Place the bowl on the floor.
2. Put on your safety goggles.

3. Use a ruler to measure a height of 6 inches (about 15 cm) above the flour's surface.

4. Release the marble into the bowl of flour. What happens when the marble strikes the surface? Does the crash kick up a ring of flour? Can you still see the marble after the impact? Record your observations. Observe the width of the crater. Is the rim of the crater high enough to be measured?

5. Over a different part of the flour, drop the second marble from a height of 1 foot (about 30 cm).

6. Examine the new crater. How does it compare with the previous one?

Be a Scientist

How does the size of the marble affect the size of the crater? Make a guess and then design an experiment that would investigate this relationship.

Moon Phases

Can you match the name of the Moon phase with its appearance?

New Moon
Last quarter
First quarter
Waning crescent
Waxing crescent
Full Moon

Hint: Waxing means "growing" and waning means "shrinking."

LUNAR CYCLE

Every twenty-eight days the Moon circles the Earth. It's this movement (against a mostly fixed direction of sunlight) that explains the phases of the Moon. Confused? Perhaps this activity might show you the light? (Or, more appropriately, the lack of light.)

In a darkened room, turn on a television or computer monitor. The TV plays the role of the Sun. Stand in the middle of the room.

Answer on page 79.

With your arm extended, hold out a small ball. The ball represents the Moon while you represent Earth.

Which side of the ball is the light falling on? If the ball isn't positioned in your shadow, half of its surface will be lit. However, depending upon where the ball is, the amount of light on the surface that you see changes.

This is what happens during the phases of the Moon. As the Moon's position changes, Earthly observers get a different view of the lunar surface.

Impress Ye Olde English Teacher

The word "lunatic" has a lunar connection. Centuries ago, people observed a greater number of people who acted insane during the time of a full Moon.

Shadow Games (Solar Eclipse)

During a solar eclipse, the Sun gets:

a) Eaten by a huge dragon.
b) Blown out by the solar wind.
c) Blocked out by the Moon.

ANSWER: c) Blocked out by the Moon. It's a position-thing that involves the Sun, the Moon, and the Earth. When these three bodies are in the right position, the Moon blocks out the Sun's surface. Without sunlight, we're in the dark.

Although the darkness isn't permanent, it's enough to scare people. Back in the Dark Ages, some people thought that this signaled the end of the world. Others believed that the Sun was being eaten by a monster. Still others thought that the royal family forgot to pay the electric bill—the *BIG* electric bill.

MODEL AN ECLIPSE

You'll Need
Plastic foam ball   Flashlight
Stick   Globe*

*The globe is not necessary. It does, however, make this a much cooler-looking activity.

Penumbra

Umbra

1. Insert the stick into the plastic foam ball so that it can be a handle.
2. Position the ball (which represents the Moon) in front of the globe. If you don't have a globe, you can use a map or even a plain old tabletop.
3. Turn on the flashlight. Aim the beam at the Moon so that its shadow is cast upon the Earth's surface. The place where the shadow falls experiences an eclipse.

TWO SHADOWY TYPES

Examine any shadow and you'll uncover two parts. The inner shadow is dark and complete. Scientists call this the umbra (UM-bra). Surrounding the umbra is an outer partial shadow. This shadow is much lighter. Scientists call this partial shadow the penumbra (PEN-um-bra).

TOTAL SOLAR ECLIPSE

From within the umbra, the total solar eclipse looks like this:

That black spot is the Moon covering up the Sun's disk. The bright rays are the Sun's outer atmosphere.

SAFETY FIRST
Never look at an eclipse (not even through sunglasses)! The light that reaches your eyes can cause permanent blindness. There are special viewing glasses for looking at solar eclipses. Ask an adult to help you find a pair.

Wanderers

Imagine living a couple of thousand years ago. Each evening you look up and see an incredible pattern of twinkling lights. A few of these lights catch your attention. Unlike the others that remain fixed within the pattern of stars, these lights don't stay in the same place. The move isn't *major*. In fact, you hardly recognize it from evening to evening. However, over months of sky watching a cool pattern emerges. These points of light follow a looping path as they travel across the sky.

Path of Mars

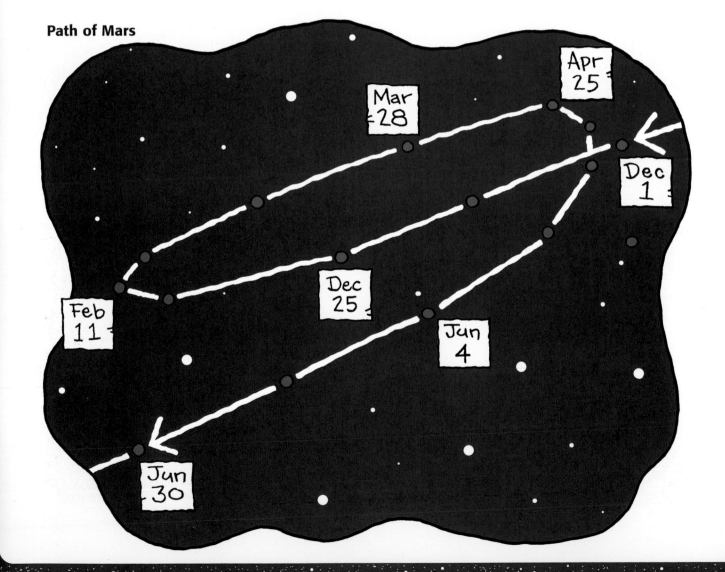

The Greeks called them *planets*. The word "planet" comes from *plantos*, the Greek word for wanderers. To them (and other cultures), planets were special stars that wandered across an unchanging pattern.

FIND THE WANDERER

It's time to find a wanderer. Check out these from drawings of the nighttime sky. Each one was made on a different night. Can you uncover any planets?

Answer on page 79.

Squished Circles

Most planets have a path called an orbit that most closely resembles which of these two shapes?

a) Circle.

b) Ellipse (squished circle).

ANSWER: a) Circle. The orbits of most planets are almost perfect circles.

But you might be wondering, "What? How can that be? My science teachers told me that the orbits were ellipses. What's going on?"

Your teachers were right. The orbits are ellipses (e-LIP-seas). However, they are only slightly flattened. In fact, the squish is so small that unless someone told you about it, you probably wouldn't realize it was there.

However, when we're discussing comets, the ellipse takes on a much more stretched (and elliptical) shape. Therefore, a comet's orbit actually looks like the ellipse shown here.

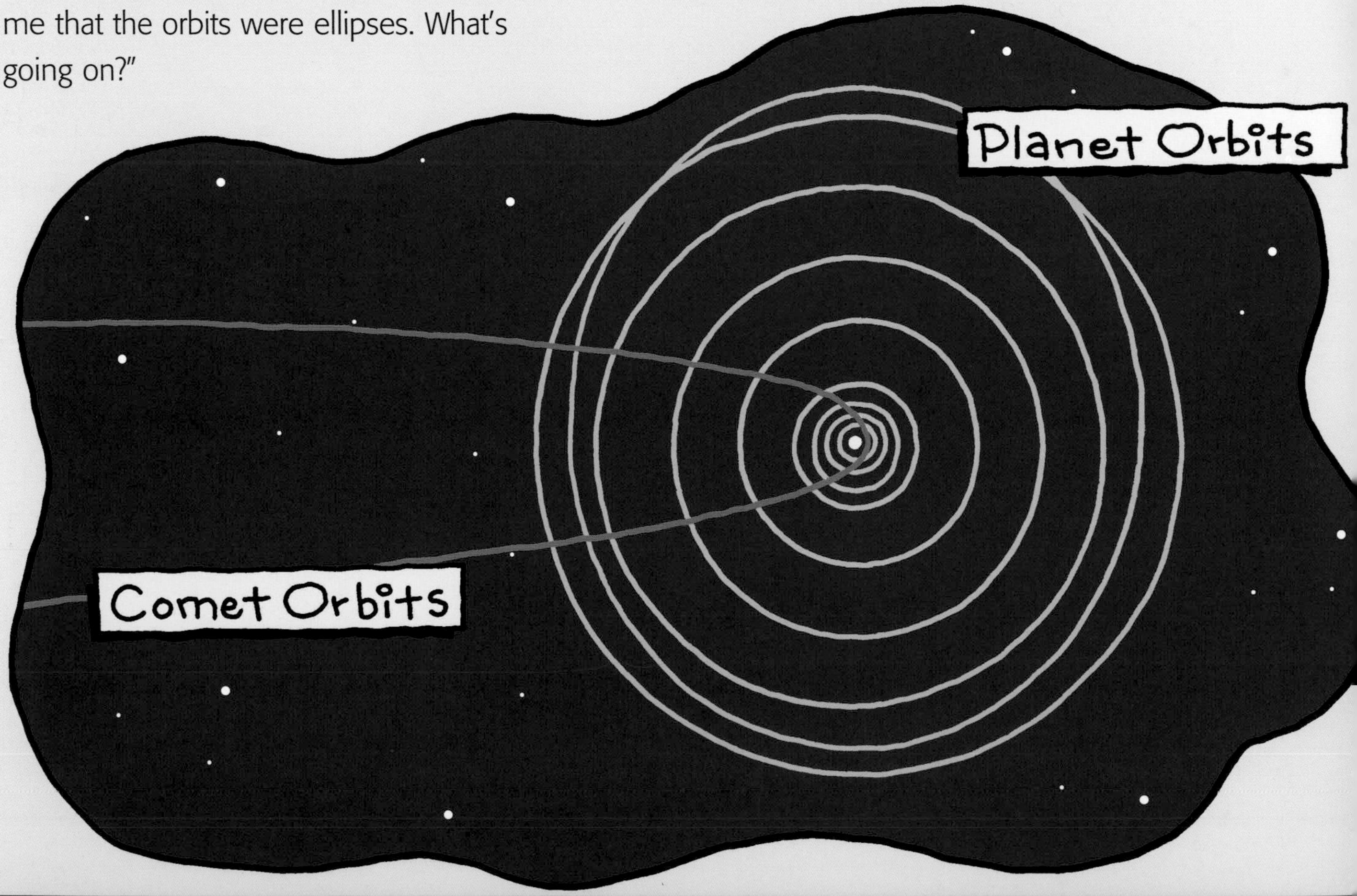

Planet Orbits

Comet Orbits

MAKE AN ELLIPSE

Here's a cool way to impress your math and science teacher. All you need are two pushpins, string, pencil, blank paper, and an old packing box.

1. Tear off a large scrap of cardboard from an old packing box.
2. Place a sheet of blank paper on top of the cardboard.
3. Insert two pushpins through the paper and into the cardboard. The pins should be in the center of the board about a thumb's length apart.
4. Tie the string into a loop.
5. Place the loop over the two pushpins.
6. Position your pencil inside the loop. Slide the pencil away from the pushpins so that the string is kept tight.
7. Slowly move the pencil across the paper while keeping the loop tight at all times. When you are done, examine the shape you have created. It's an ellipse.

Inner Planets

The four planets closest to the Sun are called the inner planets. All of these "wanderers" have hard, rocky surfaces. Even Earth has a hard surface beneath its mostly ocean-covered exterior.

The four inner planets have other similarities. Beneath their hard exterior, they have a liquid core made of melted metal. These planets also have few or no Moons.

How well do you know the inner planets? Match the planet with its unique feature.

Mercury   Earth

Venus   Mars

Water World. Unlike all other planets in the solar system, this one has water that exists as a gas, liquid, and solid. It is this feature, along with the presence of an atmosphere, that explains its ability to support life.

Hot Stuff. Although this planet isn't the closest to the Sun, it is the hottest. Go figure. Its extreme temperature is the result of an atmosphere containing mostly carbon dioxide. Like a thick wool blanket, this covering traps the Sun's energy and drives surface temperatures up to over 900°F (482°C).

Old Rusty. This planet has a surface that contains plenty of iron. It also has an atmosphere that contains oxygen. Mix iron and oxygen together and what do you get? Rust.

Night and Day. It has a surface of extremes. The half of the planet that faces the Sun roasts at a constant 800°F (427°C). Better eat your ice cream quick. The half that faces away is in a super deep freeze at −270°F (−168°C).

Answers on page 79.

Outer Planets

The five planets farthest from the Sun are called the outer planets. Four of these planets have very similar features. They are Jupiter, Saturn, Uranus, and Neptune. All of these planets are made mostly of gas. As you drop through the atmosphere, the gases get thicker and thicker. Eventually, the gas gets so thick that it behaves more like marshmallow fluff than something you could inhale. At the core, the planet is solid rock.

The ninth planet is called Pluto. Unlike the other outer planets, Pluto is not made of gas nor is it very big. It is a tiny, frigid planet that may have once been a Moon of Neptune.

Equal time for outer planets. Match each outer planet with its unique feature.

Jupiter   Neptune
Saturn   Pluto
Uranus

Out of Line. Okay, so who knocked over this planet's spin? Instead of spinning like a top as it orbits the Sun, this planet spins on its side.

Old Stormy. This planet has a storm that could swallow up several Earths! Get the picture? It's a big storm. Along with the planet's bands and violent atmosphere, it has awesome lightning bolts that can fry an entire city!

Famous Ringer. Most of the outer planets have some sort of rings. This one, however, wins "best in show." The rings are formed from chunks of rock and space dust that circle this planet. Some people think that the system of rings is all that is left from a Moon that was destroyed in a gigantic collision.

An Outsider. This outsider is *really* an outsider. It just doesn't fit into the plan. It should be a gas giant like the other outer planets but instead it's a faraway, rocky runt.

Occasional Outsider. For most of the time, this gaseous giant is next to the last planet in our system. However, every couple of hundred years, this plant becomes the most distant wanderer of our system.

Answers on page 79.

Leftovers Anyone?

Midway between the orbits of Mars and Jupiter is an area called the asteroid (AS-ter-oid) belt. Here, thousands of large space rocks called asteroids follow a planet-like orbit around the Sun. Many scientists think that these rocks were leftovers from the cloud of dust that formed our Sun and planets. These leftovers never came together into a complete planet when the nine planets formed.

A Model System

To get a better feel for our solar system, let's build a model. The best model shows the relative planet size and the distance of each planet to the Sun. However, when we reduced the size of our Earth to a pinhead, Pluto was out in left field—literally. For our model, the correct distance of our Pluto to the Sun would mean that you would have to place Pluto about 560 feet (170 m) away!

So we rethought the model idea and decided to break it into two separate activities. The modeling you'll do here will show you the relative sizes of the nine planets. The following spread will model the distances of the planets' orbits.

MAKING A MODEL

The cutouts that you'll make will show the relative size of the disk of each planet. To make things easier, we approximated their measurements, so don't be upset if they don't match up perfectly with the real ones.

To build these disks, you'll need a drawing compass, construction paper, and scissors. Colorful markers can also be used to identify the planets, draw some cool surface features, and list some facts about these sky objects.

Planet	Scaled Planet Width
Mercury	0.4 in. (1 cm)
Venus	1 in. (2.5 cm)
Earth	1 in. (2.5 cm)
Mars	.5 in. (1.3 cm)
Jupiter	11 in. (28 cm.)
Saturn	9 in. (23 cm)
Uranus	4 in. (10 cm)
Neptune	3.5 in. (9 cm)
Pluto	0.2 in. (0.5 cm)

SUNNY COMPARISON

If you want to include a Sun cutout in the same size scale, you'll need to cut out a disk that has a width of about 110 in. (2794 cm).

Make a Mobile

You could make a cool planetary mobile using these measurements. The extra materials you'll need are string, tape, and straws from which to hang the planet cutouts. Figure out the best way to balance the cutouts and then hang the mobile up in your room.

Distances In the System

Now that you've modeled the size of planets, check out the relative distances of each planet to the Sun. We'll base our measurements on a Sun that is shrunken down to the size of a period at the end of this sentence. Even at that tiny size, our model means placing Pluto at the far end of the room!

ONE STEP BEYOND

Using the same scale as our model, the nearest star to our own Sun would be about 18 miles (29 km) away! It seems like a lot until you consider the scale distance to the center of the Milky Way Galaxy. If our Sun was scaled down to the size of a dot, our galactic center would be about 117,000 miles (188,340 km) away!

Planet	Scaled Distance Between Each Planet and the Sun*
Mercury	1.6 in. (4 cm)
Venus	3 in. (7.7 cm)
Earth	4 in. (11 cm)
Mars	6.5 in. (16 cm)
Jupiter	1 ft. 10 in. (56 cm)
Saturn	3 ft. 4 in. (1 m)
Uranus	6 ft. 9 in. (2 m)
Neptune	10 ft. 7 in. (3.2 m)
Pluto	13 ft. 11 in. (4.2 m)

*Like the chart in the previous spread, the distances are approximated to make modeling easier.

Yearly Voyages

As you might have guessed, the farther a planet is from the Sun, the longer it takes for the planet to go around it once. Here on Earth, that voyage takes about 365 days. It's called a year. Mercury circles the Sun in only 88 days. Compare that to Pluto, which takes over 90,000 days to make one complete journey around the Sun.

Black Holes

Most likely you've heard of black holes. They are the "right stuff" for inspiring awesome science-fiction stories. But do you really know the fact from the fiction?

A black hole begins as a really big star. As this star grows older, it becomes unstable and explodes in a massive blast called a supernova! Not all of the star stuff gets scattered outward by the explosion. A good deal of it moves inward and compacts into a super-concentrated core that is known as a black hole.

A typical black hole may be the size of a battleship but contain the squished matter of an entire star. This super-packed object creates an incredible gravitational field. The gravity is so intense that it traps everything, including light. Since the black hole sucks in nearby light, it remains unseen.

SEE THE BLACK HOLE?

You might be thinking, "If you can't see black holes, how do scientists know they exist?" Good question. Actually scientists don't know for certain that they exist. The evidence, however, strongly supports the existence of black holes.

Black holes suck in all sorts of things. As this stuff moves inwards, it gets squished and produces X-ray radiation. Unlike the visible light that remains trapped by the black hole's gravity, the X rays get away. Earthly observatories detect the X rays but not a visible source. This suggests that something we can't see is producing massive amounts of X rays.

Another piece of evidence comes from unusual orbits of things we do see. Instead of following a typical path, a distant star may act as if it is grabbed by a nearby star's gravity. Yet there is no nearby star—or at least one that is visible.

WARP SPEED

You can get a feel for how a black hole warps space using a piece of stretchy nylon material, a ruler, marker, rubber band, large can, and a round paperweight. Lay out a square of the stretchy material on a table. Use the ruler and marker to create a grid of vertical and horizontal lines.

Place the marked fabric over the mouth of the can. Use a rubber band to secure it in place. Now, place the paperweight in the center of the fabric. See how it distorts the grid lines. Scientists believe that like this weight, a black hole warps the space surrounding it. Straight lines and paths don't exist. Instead, things are leaning along a curve that is shaped by the black hole's intense gravity!

What's a Kid to Do?

It's 5000 years ago. You're a kid and it's time for some evening entertainment. What do you watch?

a) Black and white TV.
b) Nothing.
c) The sky.

a) Wrong. Although a black and white TV seems old, it's not that old. Actually, it became a hot item back in the 1950s, which is kind of ancient, but not on the scale we are talking about.

b) Come on, you have to watch something! You're a kid.

c) That's it. Sky watching is the fad. It offers a changing scene throughout the night. It's a great source of wild sky stories. You can use it as a clock or a calendar. Plus, if you're bright, you know how to read the sky to find out where you are—and where you're not.

EAST SIDE, WEST SIDE, SAME STORY

Although ancient societies were spread across the globe, they had a common bond—no TV. It was awful. They did, however, have a sky packed with entertainment. There were stars, planets, eclipses, comets, and phases of the Moon. Plus, watching the sky was free with no monthly fees or commercials!

In Egypt, careful attention was paid to a star called Sirius. There is a natural timing of this star's rise in the summer sky to the flooding of the Nile. By predicting flooding (and not telling how), royal families and priests appeared to have magical powers.

←Sirius

I predict the Nile will now flood!

In the Americas, the Mayans and Aztecs believed that the stars affected all parts of everyday life. They built huge pyramids and calendars to worship the gods and their places in the sky.

In China, eclipses were feared. In order to prevent the Sun from being swallowed by a dragon, people beat gongs to frighten the dragon away. Since it helped to know when your drumming would be needed, the Chinese became skilled at predicting eclipses.

SOLVE A MYSTERY

The ancient Egyptians didn't have compasses. Yet, many of their pyramids were built so that the sides were perfectly lined up with north, south, east, and west. How did they do it? Did some alien super-culture point out the directions—or was it something more "down to Earth"?

Answer page 79.

Dividing Up the Sky

The sky is a big place. In order to make sense of its overwhelming splattering of stars, you need to divide it into regions. The ancient sky-watchers split the sky into areas called constellations (con-ste-LAY-shuns). Like naming a building after a statesperson, the constellations were named after gods or figures in their myth and culture.

Since many constellations appear at only certain times of the year, they are perfect reminders for seasonal events such as flooding, harvesting, and planting. Knowing the position of a constellation helped you manage life!

PATTERNS

As you might imagine, different cultures saw different things in the patterns of stars. Check out these stars below. Suppose you had to identify the pattern as some sort of familiar shape. What might it be?

Native Americans and the ancient Greeks thought this pattern represented a bear. The Egyptians viewed it as part of a bull. The Chinese thought it represented a sky chariot. Today, we call this constellation the Great Bear. Astronomers recognize eighty-eight different constellations. Each is identified by a Latin name. The Great Bear is called Ursa Major. Can you imagine a bear's body highlighted by these stars? Perhaps connecting the dots make it easier to see?

Nice Tale

Bears don't have long tails. The Native Americans interpreted those extra stars as hunters following the bear.

Dipper in a Bear

Look at the back and the tail of the Great Bear. Hidden within this pattern of stars is perhaps *the* most familiar sky shape. It's called the Big Dipper. The Big Dipper is formed by seven bright stars that seem to outline the shape of a kitchen serving spoon.

The North Star

For those of you who live north of the equator, there's a special star seen in the nighttime sky. Polaris (po-LAIR-is), also known as the North Star, is unlike all other stars in the northern sky. That's because as the night goes on, Polaris remains in one place. All other stars appear to move in circular paths around Polaris.

You can picture the movement of nighttime stars by imagining the sky as a cosmic record on a huge turntable. Place Polaris at the center of the turntable. In your mind, slowly spin the sky. Polaris stays put while the other stars move around it. It takes 24 hours for the sky to complete one spin. (Actually, it's the Earth that is spinning, but you get the point.)

Impress An Adult

The point in the sky that appears to stay put while the rest of the sky spins is called the *celestial pole*. In the northern sky, Polaris is located at this pole.

FINDING POLARIS

There are several ways to find Polaris. Perhaps the easiest way to locate this star is to first find the Big Dipper. Remember, the Big Dipper is located in the Great Bear constellation.

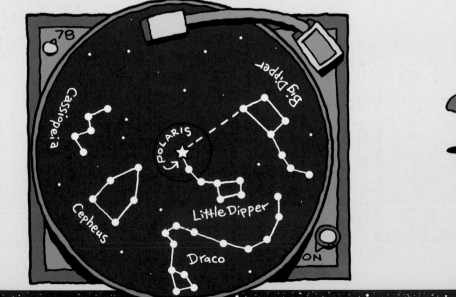

Look into the nighttime sky. You shouldn't have any problem finding the Big Dipper. Once you see it, identify its two pointer stars, Dubhe and Merak. A line drawn through both stars "points" to Polaris.

The distance from Dubhe to Polaris can be measured by a spread of fingers. Hold your hand up to the sky. Extend your thumb and little finger. Polaris is about the same distance as the spread from the tip of your little finger to the tip of your thumb.

LITTLE DIPPER

Polaris is in its own, but less obvious, constellation called the Little Bear, or Ursa Minor. Like the larger bear, this pattern of stars also resembles a dipper. The North Star is located at the tip of the dipper's handle. The six other stars trace out the little dipper's cup and handle. If you look at it as the Little Bear, the stars for the handle can be seen as the animal's tail while the cup is found in the bear's body.

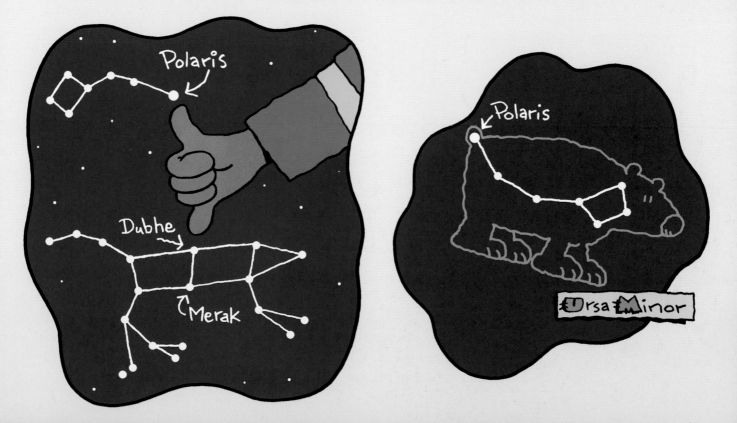

Bedroom Constellations

Before going outside to view constellations, it helps to know what you are looking for. In this activity, you'll build a star projector that will help you learn about the evening sky in your own bedroom.

You'll Need
Flashlight
Round oatmeal box
Scissors
Construction paper
Ruler
Pushpin
Tape
Stack of old newspapers

1. Ask an adult to cut away a large circle in the center of the oatmeal box bottom. It is important that she doesn't cut the entire bottom out. She should leave an edge on which to tape your star cutouts.
2. Cut a hole in the lid of your oatmeal box. The hood of your flashlight should fit into this hole.
3. Use tape to secure this cover to the flashlight hood.
4. Copy or trace any of the constellation patterns shown on the opposite page onto pieces of construction paper.
5. Make a circle around each constellation you've copied by tracing the round bottom of the oatmeal box over it. Use your scissors to cut out each circle.
6. Place the cutout constellation on a stack of old newspapers. Carefully use your pushpin to punch a hole at the position of each star.
7. Use tape to attach the cutout to the bottom end of the oatmeal box.
8. While holding the flashlight, attach the lid to the box.
9. Switch on the flashlight and dim the lights in the room. What do you see?

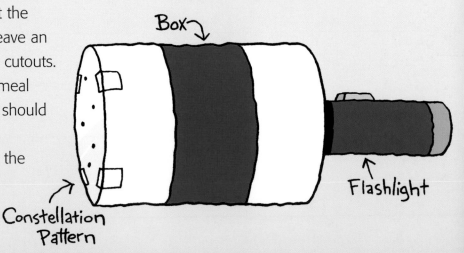

Box

Flashlight

Constellation
Pattern

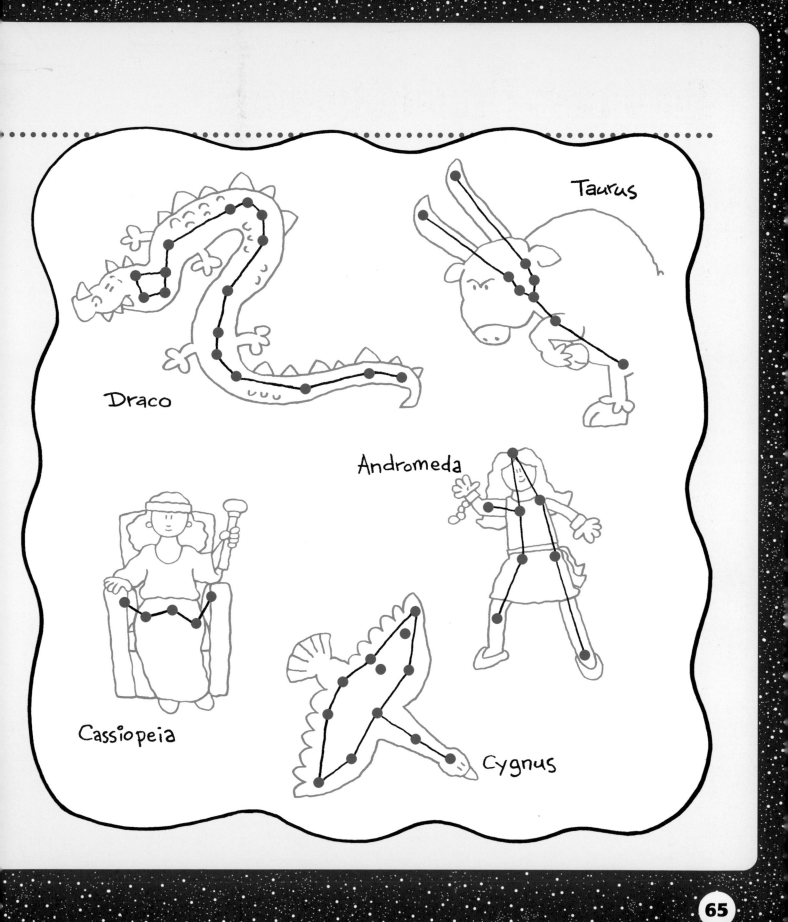

Taurus

Draco

Andromeda

Cassiopeia

Cygnus

Finding Constellations

Now let's step outside. It's time to locate constellations. We'll focus on the star groups that are closest to Polaris.

To begin using this map as a guide, first locate the Big Dipper (in Ursa Major) in the sky. Once you uncover the Big Dipper, use the trick you learned on page 63 to find Polaris.

Look at the sky map on the opposite page. Match the overhead positions of the Big Dipper and Polaris to their placement on this map. You'll find it easiest if you rotate this map to match the sky positions. The rest is easy. To uncover locations of other constellations, just match them up to their printed placement on the sky map.

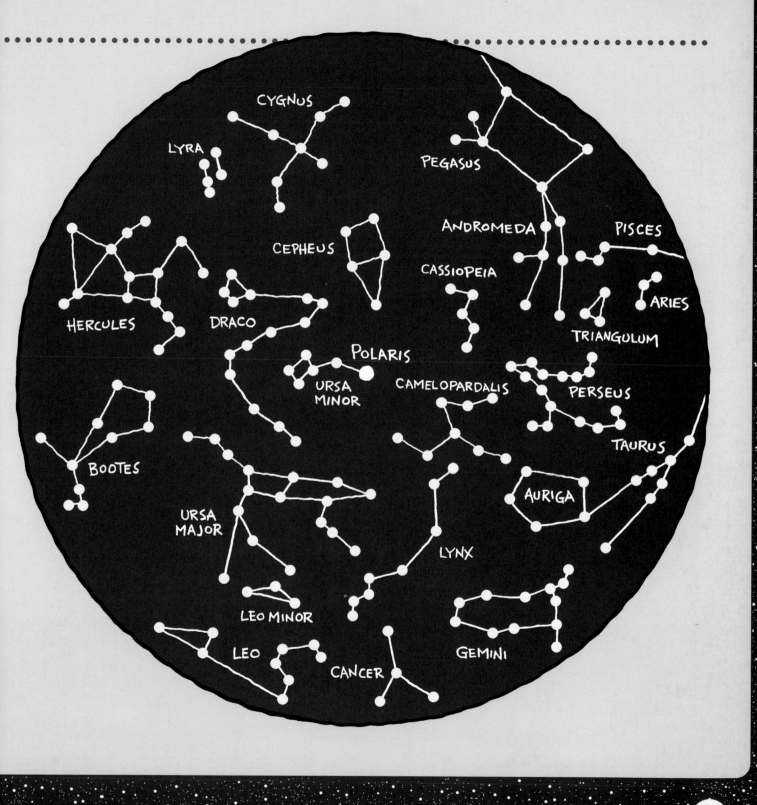

Stars Down Under

What do people living in the Southern Hemisphere see when they look into the nighttime sky?

Answer: Southern constellations. About thirty constellations belong to the sky of the Southern Hemisphere. Like people in the Northern Hemisphere, you can sometimes see some of these constellations from either side of the equator. It all depends upon the season, where you are on either side of the equator, and the constellation's distance to the celestial pole.

SOUTHERN CROSS

If you're in Florida, you can catch a glimpse of Crux, the Southern Cross. Although Crux won't be rising much above the horizon, you'll still recognize its bright and intense pattern.

But don't expect anything big. The Southern Cross is the smallest constellation in the sky. However, the Southern Cross is made up of four very bright stars. Connect the dots and the pattern forms a cross that "points" south.

During the Age of Discovery, European explorers "rediscovered" this constellation. Since the southern sky did not have a "stay-in-one-place" star like Polaris, sailors realized the value of the Southern Cross. It was their compass in the sky.

Australian Flag

The pattern of stars found on the right half of the Australian flag is the Southern Cross. Crux has also earned a place on the flags of other countries such as Brazil and New Zealand.

G'day Mate!

Moving On

As you know, the Earth doesn't spin in place. It circles the Sun at a speed of over 50,000 miles per hour (over 80,000 km/hr). This means your view into space is constantly changing. Each night, the position from which you view the stars changes by over 1,000,000 miles (1,609,000 km)!

Although we move a great distance, our view into the distant nighttime sky changes gradually. Over time, however, some constellations will completely disappear from view while others will rise above the horizon.

Because of this change, astronomers group constellations by season. There are winter, spring, summer, and fall constellations.

CIRCUMPOLAR CONSTELLATIONS

There are certain constellations that you can see throughout the year in either the Northern or Southern Hemisphere. These constellations are called circumpolar (sir-come-PO-lar) constellations.

In the Northern Hemisphere, the circumpolar constellations include: Ursa Major, Draco, Cepheus, and Cassiopeia. In the Southern Hemisphere, Crux, Hydrus, and Centaurus are some of the constellations you can see year-round.

CHARTING THE CHANGE

You can chart the "rise" and "fall" of constellations using transparency sheets (see-through plastic sheets teachers use with overhead projectors), colored markers, tape, and a window with a view of the nighttime sky.

1. Tape a transparency sheet to the inside of the window.
2. Pick a constellation or star pattern that you can see through the plastic sheet. Select one color marker. Use it to place a dot at the position of each star on your transparency sheet.
3. Note the time. On the following evening at the same time, find those same stars. Use a different colored marker to record their position.
4. Keep recording the changing position over the week. The movement that you track is caused by the Earth's advance along its orbit.

Flashes of Light

What falls to Earth during a rainstorm?

a) Water.
b) Tiny pieces of space rock.

ANSWER: Both **a** and **b.** Water is obvious. If you hadn't noticed, that's why you get wet. But pieces of space rock are the lesser-known ingredient of a rainstorm. These tiny specks of rock are called micrometeorites (MY-crow-ME-tee-ore-ites). Smaller than a grain of sand, these specks are all that's left from a meteor shower. They are the remains of larger rocks that burned up in the Earth's atmosphere. Micrometeorites are light enough to be kept in the air by breezes in the clouds. They stay there until rainstorms flush these particles out of the sky and bring them to the ground.

SHOOTING STARS: THE REAL STORY

Shooting stars aren't stars at all. They are quick flashes of light that streak across the sky. Scientists call the streaks of light meteors. These flashes are produced when space rocks burn up in the Earth's atmosphere. Nobody sets fire to these rocks. The fire comes from the heat produced as the rock rubs against particles of air.

If the rock is large enough, some of it survives. Scientists call these earthly remains of space rock meteorites (ME-tee-or-ites). Although the famous meteorites are large hunks of rock, most are hardly visible.

OIDS TOO

A meteoroid (ME-tee-oh-royd) is the name of the space rock *before* it produces the meteor. In goes the meteoroid. It collides with air particles to produce the meteor flash. Then out comes the meteorite.

MARTIAN METEORITES

Of the more than 20,000 meteorites found on Earth, scientists think that a few dozen of them came from the surface of Mars. They believe that many, many years ago, an asteroid or meteoroid crashed into Mars. This impact hurled rocks into space. Some of these Martian rocks collided with Earth. The rest is history.

A Yearly Shower

Imagine running around the edge of the school playground. Round and round you go, following this circular path. Now suppose that a cloud of insects was buzzing around one part of this path. Each time you passed that cloud, you'd smash into the insects. Ugh.

Likewise, the Earth runs circles around the Sun. Each time it gets to the same point in its path, it crashes into hunks of space debris left by passing comets. These collisions produce meteor showers. Since they always occur at the same point in the Earth's orbit, we know the exact dates of these reoccurring events.

From over 1500 showers, we've listed the major ones below. They are named after the part of the sky from which they appear to come.

CATCH A METEORITE

You'll Need

A large plastic container	Distilled water
	Lint-free cloth
An adult	Magnet
Soap	Plastic bag

FAMOUS METEOR SHOWERS

Shower	Approximate number of meteors per hour	Most activity
Leonids*	15 to 150,000	Nov. 18
Quadrantids	100	Jan. 3
Persids	65	Aug. 12
Germinids	50	Dec. 6–19
Orionids	35	Oct. 21

* Every 33 years, the Earth passes into extra comet debris. In 1966, this caused the sightings to jump to 150,000 meteors per hour!

1. Find the next major meteor shower listed on the table to the left. On the day before the shower, have an adult set up a large plastic container in an open and safe area. The location should be an out-of-the-way spot so that the container won't be disturbed by anyone.

NOTE: Since water contains small amounts of iron material, you'll need to be sure that the container is clean. Wash it well with soap and distilled water. Then dry the container with a lint-free cloth.

2. Keep the container outside and undisturbed until after a rainstorm. Don't be discouraged if it doesn't rain on the day of the meteor shower. Anytime soon afterward will flush out the new specks of space rock that are floating around in the clouds above.

3. After the rainstorm, test the water for iron meteorites. Put a strong magnet in a plastic bag and pass the bag through the water. Any iron particles that fell in the rain will stick to the magnet. Although some of the iron particles will have an "Earthly" origin, others will be the remains of space rocks. With your teacher's permission, bring these tiny space rocks to school and examine them under a microscope!

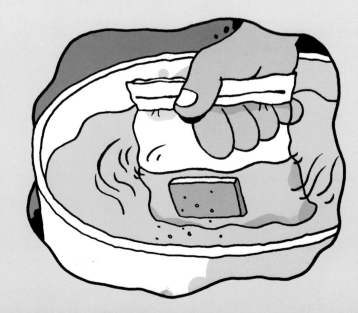

Blowing in the Wind

A comet's tail stretches out from the:

a) Back end of the comet.
b) Front end of the comet.

ANSWER: How about **a** and **b**? You see, it all depends. Although it makes sense to think of a tail on the back end, that's not always the case when it comes to comets. The comet's tail is a mix of comet pieces (ice, dirt, water vapor) that are blowing in the wind—the solar wind, that is. The Sun's radiation slams into the comet and spreads the tail in the opposite direction.

COMET COMMENTS AND CONTENTS

Scientists think that a whole bunch of comet wannabes exist beyond the orbit of Pluto. They are found in a region of space called the *Oort Cloud*. Most of the time, these comets are happy just hanging out in this distant region of space.

Then, it happens. What happens? No one knows for sure, but something occurs that sends a comet on a course towards the Sun. As it approaches the Sun, the comet becomes visible. Nothing magical—it's purely a physical change. When sunlight strikes the comet, it lights up and begins to break down. As the comet falls apart, its pieces are carried off by the solar wind.

Approaching Sun

Moving Away from Sun

IT'S A BREEZE

With the help of an adult and a portable fan, you can model what happens as a comet moves through the solar wind. Attach a streamer or strip of tissue paper to a ruler. Everyone puts on safety goggles.

Turn on the fan. Walk along your comet's path. As you move, the adult keeps aiming the blast of air directly at the streamer. Notice how your comet tail's direction depends upon the breeze, not your movement.

The Final Frontier

So what's the future of our universe? Nobody really knows. Since our understanding of the universe is incomplete, space scientists don't know if the universe will keep expanding or, at some point, start shrinking. It all depends upon how much matter is out there. If enough of it exists, then gravity will pull everything together and eventually shrink the universe. If not, the universe will keep expanding forever.

In the meantime, astronomers continue to study the sky—either through telescopes on Earth or through those that have been launched into space, like the Hubble Space Telescope. Astronauts keep going into space and will someday explore other planets. Who knows, maybe you'll find yourself working aboard an orbiting space-station or setting foot on the surface of Mars?

Answers

MEET THE MOON

c. Our Sun has never had a sister—evil or otherwise. The rocks collected by astronauts who visited the Moon suggest that the Moon was once a part of the Earth. If so, it was cut loose during a really big collision between the Earth and some large chunk of space debris.

WHAT'S A KID TO DO?

The Egyptians positioned the sides of the pyramids based upon the apparent rising (east) and setting (west) of the Sun.

INNER PLANETS

Mercury – Night and Day
Venus – Hot Stuff
Earth – Water World
Mars – Old Rusty

OUTER PLANETS

Jupiter – Old Stormy
Saturn – Famous Ringer
Uranus – Out of Line
Neptune – Occasional Outsider
Pluto – An Outsider

WANDERERS

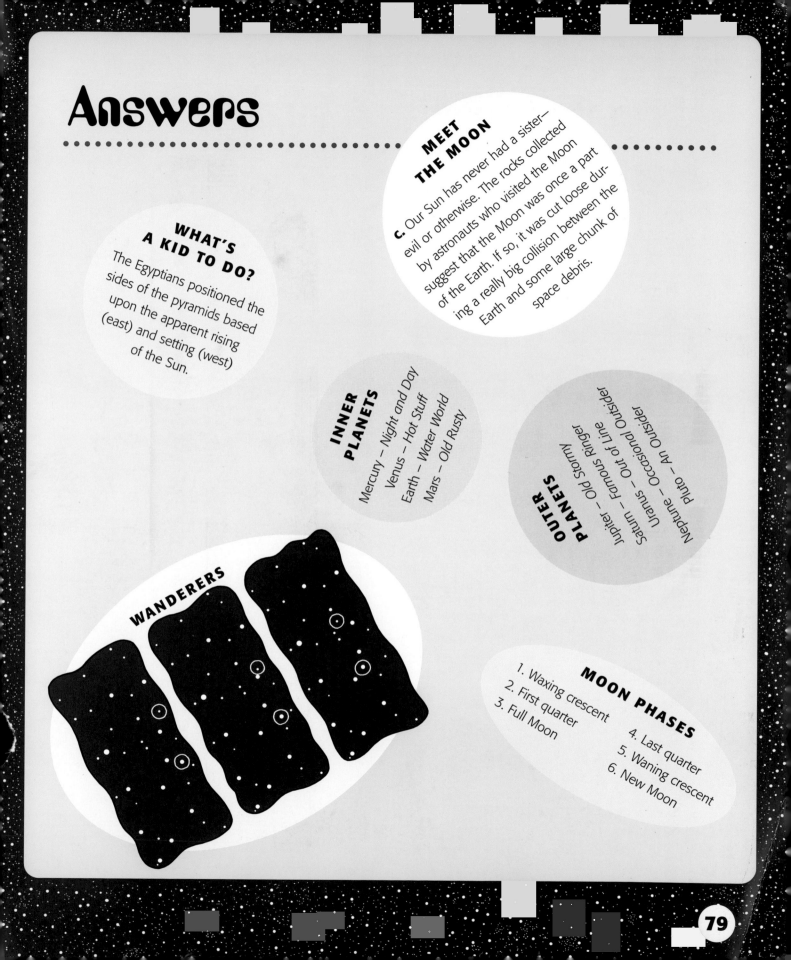

MOON PHASES

1. Waxing crescent
2. First quarter
3. Full Moon
4. Last quarter
5. Waning crescent
6. New Moon

About the Author

Michael Anthony DiSpezio is a renaissance educator who teaches, writes, and conducts teacher workshops throughout the world. He is the author of *Critical Thinking Puzzles*, *Great Critical Thinking Puzzles*, *Challenging Critical Thinking Puzzles*, *Visual Thinking Puzzles*, *Awesome Experiments in Electricity and Magnetism*, *Awesome Experiments in Force and Motion*, *Awesome Experiments in Light and Sound*, *Optical Illusion Magic*, *Simple Optical Illusion Experiments with Everyday Materials*, *Eye-Popping Optical Illusions*, *Map Mania*, *Dino Mania*, *Weather Mania*, and *Super Sensational Science Fair Projects* (all from Sterling). He is also the co-author of over two dozen elementary, middle, and high school science textbooks and has been a "hired creative-gun" for clients including The Weather Channel and Children's Television Workshop. He also develops activities for the classroom guides to *Discover* magazine and *Scientific American Frontiers*.

Michael was a contributor to the National Science Teachers Association's Pathways to Science Standards. This document set offers guidelines for moving the national science standards from vision to practice. Michael's work with the NSTA has also included authoring the critically acclaimed NSTA curriculum, *The Science of HIV*. These days, Michael is the curriculum architect for the JASON Academy, an on-line university that offers professional development courses for science teachers.

To learn more about this topic and Michael's cool science activities, log on to www.Awesomescience.org.

Index